Hysterical Alph[abet]
Alphabets, Characters and [...]

Written and Illustrated by Kim L. Savage

This book is dedicated to
my children, whom I anticipate,
my mother and grandmother.

Published by Kim Savage Press
Lots of Fun and Education Curriculum

Copyright 2015 Kim L. Savage

All rights reserved worldwide. No part of this book may be reproduced or transmitted in any form or by any means electronic or mechanical, including photocopying, recording or by any information storage and retrieval system without written permission from Kim L. Savage.

Printed in the United States of America
ISBN: 978-0-578-16806-7

1. Children's Book 2. Educational
HYSTERICAL ALHABETICALS
Alphabets, Characters and Rhymes

Written and Illustrated by Kim L. Savage

The purpose of this book is to educate and entertain.

Introduction

Welcome to the funny and imaginative world of the **Hysterical Alphabeticals.** Meet Adams Apple, Bubble Boy, Coconut Cloud, Hairy Hero, Popcorn Pilot, Uncle Uranus and many more zany characters. Read about Eddie Egg who tells of having a family of eleven and learns from Humpty Dumpty not to sit up on a wall. Take a trip with Popcorn Pilot as he flies everywhere. His popcorn kernels go up in the air. The colorful creative characters and fantasy rhymes are sure to put a smile upon your young child's face and encourage them to learn the alphabet.

This book is an educational tool that makes learning the alphabet fun and easy. It is a source that can usher young children into reading skills and also expand their vocabulary. This educational source can be used for ages three and up.

The author is currently the founder of Lots of Fun and Education, a company that furnishes family child cares with a fun and creative curriculum and also provides temporary staffing. The author has taught pre-school age children for nearly twenty years.

Aa
Adam's Apple

Adam's Apple made

Squishy, squashy, apple sauce

In his apple factory.

Cinnamon and strawberries

Are very necessary to

Spice the apple treat.

Bb
Bubble Boy

Have you ever seen a Bubble Boy before? I have!

One day he showed up at my door.

I thought he was amazing, because he did not pop!

My mom saw him and dropped her pot,

I think she was shocked.

Cc

Coconut Cloud

There's coconut juice
In the Coconut Cloud,
Making coconut rain on
A traveling plane. The plane
Is on its way to Jamaica,
It's a beautiful island.
There are coconut clouds to keep
Everyone smiling.

Dd

Darla Dish

Darla Dish took a bath in the kitchen sink.

Everyone likes a clean dish don't you think?

She borrowed bubbles from Bubble Boy

To soak herself for good;

Splish and splash, she dipped herself,

Because she knew she should.

Ee

Eddie Egg

Little Eddie Egg had a family of eleven.

The youngest of the bunch,

Eddie Egg was only seven.

He learned from Humpty Dumpty

Not to sit up on a wall.

He didn't sit on top of anything,

Because he didn't want to fall.

Ff
Fried Fish

Two fish, grey fish, frying in a pan;

One named Stan, the other one Dan;

Crispy, crunchy, good and munchy,

Perfect breakfast, dinner or lunchy.

Gg

Giant Girl

In a far away land lived a Giant Girl;

From where she stood she could view the world;

Although she was huge she was never a bully;

Only shared everything from dolls to jelly.

Hh

Harry Hero

Not many years ago,

Came the rise of Harry Hero;

He has power to defeat criminals

And overcome any obstacle;

He uses super hair to tangle up his enemy,

Every battle for Harry Hero ends in victory.

Ii

Igloo Ice Cream

My Igloo Ice Cream is a tasty dessert,

I like it on a cone and not all over my shirt.

Jj
Jelly Jar

I jump for joy for strawberry jelly,

In my Jelly Jar;

I want it in my belly,

I think it's the best by far.

Kind Kim

Kind Kim has a good heart;

One day she chose to build a park;

A place where children could come and play,

With mom and dad on Saturday.

Ll

Lollipop Linda

Lollipop Linda is as sweet as can be;

Her grandmother Tweet owned

A candy shop on Lemon Drop Street;

When the children were good

Granny gave them a prize,

Rainbow colored lollipops

Would give them bright eyes.

Mm
Movie Mom

I woke up one morning and who did I see?

Movie Mom of course, she was on tv!

I was quite entertained by what I saw,

Something about a lion and a thorn

Mom pulled from his paw.

Nn

Nancy Necklace

Put her on your neck and look glamorous;

Every girl should have a Nancy Necklace;

In a treasure box deep in the Evergreens,

I found Nancy Necklace right there sparkling.

Oo

Oscar Oyster

Oscar Oyster lives in a shell;

Oscar Oyster has no tail;

He's a private animal with not much to say;

At the bottom of the ocean he wants to stay.

Pp
Popcorn Pilot

Popcorn Pilot flying everywhere;

Popcorn kernels up in the air;

Have a safe trip to the other side;

Popcorn Pilot have a smooth ride.

Qq

Quarter Queen

The Quarter Queen ruled her kingdom

In great excellence;

Her guest would say about her castle

That it's magnificent;

The queen was good

To the people in her kingdom;

Quarters they would give,

And trusted her to lead them.

Rr
Rock Radio

Tip, tip, boom,

Tip, tip, cack,

Hey Rock Radio I like that;

How many songs will you play?

Rock Radio I can dance all day.

Ss

Slimy Stuff

Slimy Stuff on the door;

Slimy Stuff on the floor;

I have Slimy stuff on my hands,

Because I was putting slimy stuff in a can;

My dad said I can't go outside to play ball,

Until I clean Slimy Stuff off of my wall.

Tt

Two T-Shirts

Two T-Shirts, free t-shirts
In my store today;
Take your pick you can choose
The blue or the grey;
It doesn't matter which one you pick
All my shirts will fit;
It's funny how one size fits all
And the fabric doesn't itch.

Uu

Uncle Uranus

My Uncle Uranus saw the strangest

Thing on Saturday,

But what could be so strange

Out there in outer space?

All I ever see is darkness and stars,

But he wrote me a letter saying that

He saw a duck on mars.

Vv

Victory Venus

Victory Venus has good sportsmanship;

He's number one, he's confident;

He can shoot a jump shot and

A three point shot!

Victory Venus slam dunks a lot.

Ww
Winner Whale

Whistling and watching whales,

I spotted Winner Whale winning;

Swimming in the waves what a wonderful feeling;

He took a picture with trophy in hand;

He never says I can't,

And always says I can.

Xx

Xavier X-Ray

Xavier X-Ray is on like a light;

You can see his bones even at night;

He glows in the dark, he's so fun to see;

With two hundred and six bones in his body.

Yippy Yo-Yo

My name is Yippy Yo-Yo

I live in a toy store;

I have a huge family

Of a billion and four;

We come in every color

Even gold and swirl;

Yippy Yo-Yo is all over the world.

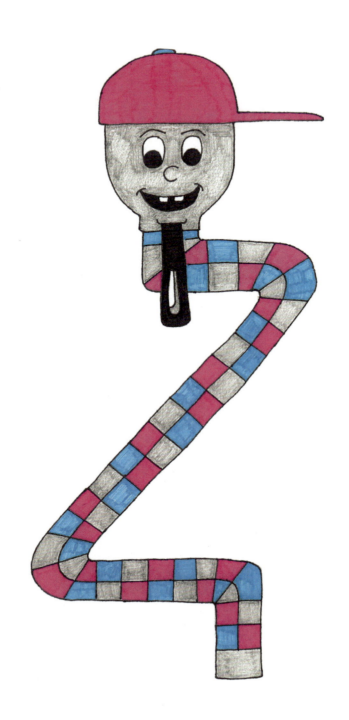

Zz

Zig Zag Zipper

ZigZag Zipper zipping left to right,

Zealous about this zipping,

He's out of sight!

Sort of like a race car

When zipping up my sweater,

I'm not cold anymore,

I feel so much better.

Made in the USA
San Bernardino, CA
04 January 2016